W9-BAG-244

SCIENCE
VS.
THE ENERGY CRISIS

by Nick Hunter

Gareth Stevens
Publishing

Please visit our website, www.garethstevens.com. For a free color catalog of all our high-quality books, call toll free 1-800-542-2595 or fax 1-877-542-2596.

Publisher Cataloging Data

Hunter, Nick
    Science vs. the energy crisis / by Nick Hunter.
p.   cm. – (Science fights back)
Includes bibliographical references and index.
Summary: This book explores the world's dependence on nonrenewable energy sources, the danger some power sources pose to the environment, and how scientists are searching for alternative forms of energy.
Contents: Energy everywhere – The energy crisis – Taking on the energy crisis – Debates and issues – The future – The fight continues : is science winning? – The energy story.
ISBN 978-1-4339-8695-6 (hard bound) – ISBN 978-1-4339-8696-3 (pbk.)
ISBN 978-1-4339-8697-0 (6-pack)
    1. Power resources—Juvenile literature   2. Power resources—Environmental aspects—Juvenile literature   3. Renewable energy resources—Juvenile literature [1. Power resources   2. Renewable energy resources]   I. Title
II. Title: Science versus the energy crisis
          2013
    333.79—dc23

First Edition

Published in 2013 by
Gareth Stevens Publishing
111 East 14th Street, Suite 349
New York, NY 10003

© 2013 Gareth Stevens Publishing

Produced by Calcium, www.calciumcreative.co.uk
Designed by Simon Borrough
Edited by Sarah Eason and Harriet McGregor

Photo credits: Dreamstime: Cheryl Casey 23, Piero Cruciatti 28b, Dtguy 24, Koi88 12, Leonidikan 20, Liumangtiger 14, Dimitar Marinov 26, Petemasty 10, Luca Petruzzi 41t, Jeremy Richards 34b, Michael Shake 25, Joao Virissimo 6, Maksym Yemelyanov 13; NASA 18; Shutterstock: Africa924 34, Aslysun 29, Tomasz Bidermann 11, Darren Brode 30-31, Alexander Chaikin 22, EGD 38, Bart Everett 7, Fatseyeva 31, Jorg Hackemann 33, Kardasheva 19tl, Christopher Kolaczan 21, Michal Kowalski 3, 17, Pitsanu Kraichana 29c, Philip Lange 16, Littleny 5, Robin Lund 19, Mizio70 cover bl, Monkey Business Images 8, Olena Mykhaylova 4, Natursports 39, Thomas Nord 36, Psynovec 42-43, Sergej Razvodovskij 28t, Przemyslaw Skibinski 15, Sopotnicki 9, Spirit of America 32, Ssuaphotos cover tl, br, Kenny Tong 27t, TonyV3112 36c, 43t, Triff 40.

Printed in the United States of America

CPSIA compliance information: Batch #CW13GS: For further information contact Gareth Stevens, New York, New York at 1-800-542-2595.

Contents

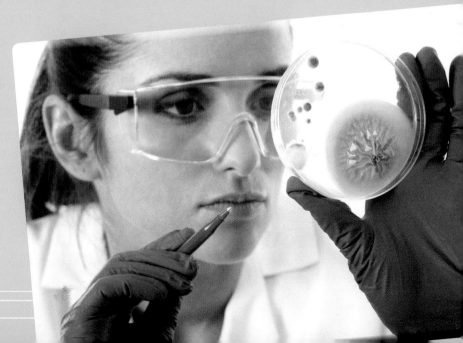

Energy Everywhere

What is the first thing you do when you wake up in the morning? Do you turn off your alarm clock? Maybe you take a shower and then rush downstairs to make breakfast? Even in these first few minutes of the day, energy is essential. Energy is needed to power the clock, heat the water for your shower, and cook your breakfast. Your body needs energy too, which it gets from the food you eat.

Energy from the Sun
Plants need energy, too. All plants, including food crops, need energy from the sun to make them grow.

FUEL FOR ENERGY

Food is the fuel for our bodies, but the gadgets and machines we use also need fuel. This fuel comes from a range of sources. Some power plants make electricity by burning coal and gas. The electricity powers lights and computers. It is carried to homes and businesses via overhead and underground power cables. Vehicles burn fuel in the form of gasoline, diesel oil, or aviation fuel.

POWER PROBLEMS

In the last 250, years humans have harnessed steam power and discovered electricity. These sources have powered the appliances and industries that have created the modern world. However, these developments have used up huge amounts of our planet's energy resources. Today we use so much fuel that the world is suffering an energy crisis. This book will look at the crisis and consider whether we can continue to use these energy resources as we have in the past. If we do, will this create problems that could affect the survival of humans, animals, and plants?

In the Ring

Scientists and inventors have always tried to harness energy sources for humans. Thomas Newcomen (1663–1729) built the first steam engines in the 1700s. They were powered by coal. His design was improved by James Watt (1736–1819). Modern scientists are developing new technologies to reduce our use of energy and find new energy sources.

Chapter One:
The Energy Crisis

Most people don't think too much about where the energy they use comes from. We flick a switch and it's there, ready to use. We have to remember to fill our cars with fuel, but we're never far from a gas station. You might hear people complaining when gas prices rise, or when they get a costly electricity bill, but we still don't have to worry about running out of energy.

RUNNING OUT TOMORROW?

The growing energy crisis means that this may not always be the case. Most of our energy comes from fossil fuels such as coal, oil, and gas. Fossil fuels have formed over millions of years from the remains of dead animals and plants. When the plants and animals died, they settled into layers in the oceans and on land. Over time, more and more layers of earth and rock formed on top of the remains. They became squashed and heated, and eventually turned into coal, oil, and gas. These are nonrenewable fuels. This means that once they are used, they can never be replaced. The world's leading industries and power plants are using more and more of these precious fuels all the time.

Constant Demand
The never-ending demand for energy is putting our planet under ever-increasing stress.

POLLUTED PLANET

There is another factor to think about in the energy crisis—the damage to the planet. Coal and oil are dug out of the ground. This mining can destroy beautiful and important animal and plant habitats. The burning and use of fuels also causes problems. Whenever a fuel is burned in a power plant or by a vehicle, gases are released into Earth's atmosphere. Scientists believe that over long periods of time this can seriously harm our health, and our planet's, too.

Winning or Losing?

We are using more and more energy. Our energy use from various fuels is now equivalent to using more than 12 billion tons (10.8 billion tonnes) of oil every year. Of all the countries in the world, the United States and China are the world's biggest users of energy.

Planet Under Pressure
The release of harmful gases into Earth's atmosphere is causing many problems. One of these is the melting of the polar ice caps at the far north of our planet.

Scarce Resources

Fossil fuels are essential in three ways. They are needed to generate electricity in power plants, for transportation, and also in industry. Coal was the fuel that powered the factories and steam trains of the Industrial Revolution. Gasoline is obtained from crude oil. It is used as fuel for cars. Oil is used to provide fuel for ships and aircraft. Today, oil accounts for 90 percent of the fuel used in transportation.

ENOUGH TO LAST?

Although coal is plentiful and there is enough oil to meet demand for many years, these fuels will not last forever. Some scientists are concerned that people are not discovering as much new oil as they have in the past. Any new oil that is being discovered is more difficult to extract. Some has been found in the Arctic and beneath the floor of the world's deep oceans.

Ancient Fuel
The gas that goes into your car comes from oil that has taken many millions of years to form.

USEFUL GAS

Natural gas is formed in a similar way to oil and the two are often found together. In the past, natural gas was thought of as simply a by-product of oil exploration and it was difficult to transport. Today it is increasingly important. Gas can be used for cooking but it can also be used in liquid form to power vehicles such as buses.

Danger Zone
Mining for fuel such as coal deep underground is expensive and dangerous.

A SECURE SUPPLY?

The largest known oil reserves are beneath the desert sands of countries around the Arabian Gulf, such as Saudi Arabia. Some oil-rich countries, such as Iraq and Libya, have been affected by conflict. Iran is also oil-rich but has a tense relationship with Western countries, including the United States. Both of these problems affect the supply and price of oil worldwide.

Winning or Losing?
Currently more than 80 percent of the energy we use comes from fossil fuels. Despite the search for new and sustainable fuel sources, scientists predict this will still be the case in 2030 unless there is a major change in global fuel usage.

Pollution Problem

The energy crisis is about much more than running out of fossil fuels. During the mining process itself, the environment is damaged. Transporting fossil fuels can cause problems, especially if there is an accident. Once the product reaches its destination, it is burned, releasing harmful fumes into the atmosphere.

HITTING THE HEADLINES

Pollution hits the headlines when there is an oil spill. Oil is spilled into the ocean during drilling accidents or when oil tankers are accidentally driven on to rocks. A sticky film of oil forms on top of the ocean and coats anything that comes into contact with it. This includes seabirds and other animals, such as sea turtles.

Breaking Through

Scientists now know that oil spills can damage wildlife long after the spill itself has been cleared up. In 2010, an explosion and fire at a drilling rig in the Gulf of Mexico caused a huge oil spill. Oil leaked from a seabed well at a rate of 1,000 to 5,000 barrels per day. The oil continued to leak for three months. It caused great damage to wildlife in the area. Even two years later, scientists discovered that dolphins were sick as a result of the huge spill.

Costly Spills
Seabirds covered in oil will die if the oil is not cleaned off quickly by rescue workers.

AIR POLLUTION

Although major oil spills are rare, pollution caused by fossil fuels happens all the time. Fumes released by power plants and cars can pollute the air. This affects the health of people traveling and working in busy cities.

Creating Acid Rain

Chemicals such as sulfur dioxide are released when coal is burned in power plants. These chemicals combine with water vapor in the air to produce acid rain. This rain can damage forests and poison rivers and lakes. Use of cleaner coal has helped to reduce acid rain in North America and Europe, but it remains a problem in many parts of the world.

Fukushima, Japan, 2011

Nuclear power plants generate electricity using radioactive uranium. Inside the power plant, tiny atoms are split. This generates huge amounts of energy. Nothing is burned and gases are not released into the atmosphere. However, if radiation escapes from the reactor, it can have serious and long-term health effects. All living things are likely to be affected in the area surrounding a power plant.

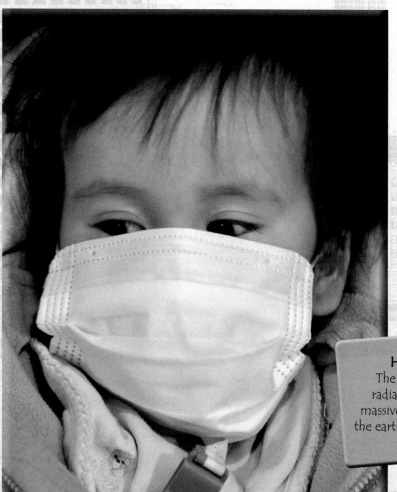

TSUNAMI STRIKE

On March 11, 2011, a massive earthquake struck off the eastern coast of Japan. This unleashed a huge wave called a tsunami. The tsunami rushed toward the coast, destroying whole towns and claiming thousands of lives. Japan is still recovering from the tsunami, which was one of the worst natural disasters in the history of the country.

Hidden Danger
The unseen threat of radiation followed the massive damage caused by the earthquake and tsunami.

HITTING FUKUSHIMA

The Fukushima nuclear power plant was directly in the path of the tsunami. The 50-foot (15-m) wave swamped the area. Three nuclear reactors lost power. This meant that the cooling systems could no longer cool the fuel inside the reactor.

NUCLEAR EMERGENCY

In the days that followed, explosions rocked the reactors, releasing radiation into the surrounding area. Anyone living within 12 miles (20 km) of the plant was evacuated. These people may never be able to return home. The authorities even considered evacuating Tokyo, the world's most populated city with almost 30 million people, but decided it wasn't necessary.

In the Ring
The power plant workers and scientists who struggled to bring the Fukushima plant under control became known as the Fukushima 50. They worked hard to cool the nuclear reactors and stop the spread of radiation. Although the brave workers wore protective clothing, their exposure to radiation could mean they will become sick in later life.

TOO RISKY?

The disaster led to a debate about nuclear power. Many felt the risks were too great to build more reactors. But people around the world also believed that burning fossil fuels could have an even greater impact.

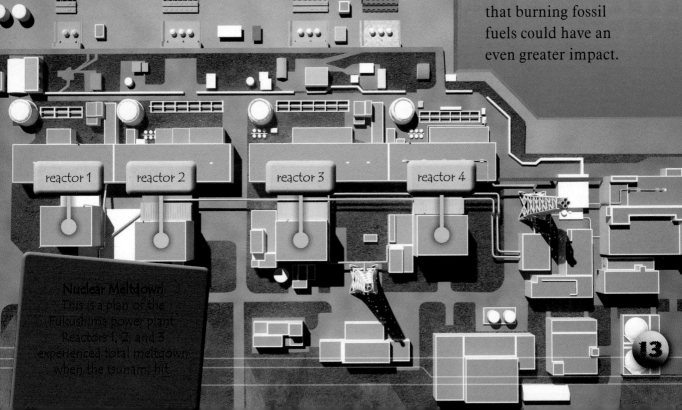

reactor 1   reactor 2   reactor 3   reactor 4

Nuclear Meltdown
This is a plan of the Fukushima power plant. Reactors 1, 2, and 3 experienced total meltdown when the tsunami hit.

Emission Emergency

The burning of fossil fuels releases harmful gases into the atmosphere. We have already seen some of the damage this pollution can cause. However, burning fossil fuels is changing Earth's atmosphere permanently.

GREENHOUSE EFFECT

The atmosphere is a layer of gases that surrounds Earth. Its gases, known as greenhouse gases, include nitrogen, oxygen, and carbon dioxide. The atmosphere protects life on Earth from some of the harmful rays in sunlight. It also acts as a blanket to trap some of the sun's energy. This system keeps the planet's surface at exactly the right temperature and is called the greenhouse effect.

CLIMATE CHANGE

Burning fossil fuels releases carbon dioxide into Earth's atmosphere. This changes the mix of gases and means that more of the sun's energy is trapped in the atmosphere. As a result, Earth's climate is becoming warmer. This gradual waming effect is called climate change.

Islands in Danger
Many tropical islands rise just a few feet above sea level. They could disappear completely if sea levels rise.

14

In the Ring

The Intergovernmental Panel on Climate Change (IPCC) studies climate change information provided by scientists around the world. In 2012, 195 countries were members of the IPCC. Every six years, the IPCC produces a report about climate change. In 2007, the IPCC predicted that Earth would see a rise in temperature of 3.2–7.2°F (1.8–4°C) by the year 2100. The next report will be published in late 2013 or early 2014.

HUGE IMPACT

The effects of climate change could be disastrous for all life on Earth. As the climate warms, parts of Earth may experience long periods of drought. Crops will suffer and animal and plant life may not be able to adapt to the new conditions and die out. Extreme weather events such as hurricanes, tornadoes, and flooding may become much more common. The polar ice caps could melt, causing sea levels to rise across the globe. Low-lying towns and cities could be flooded by seawater.

Poverty and Drought
Many of the world's poorest people live in areas where rainfall is already scarce.

Chapter Two: Taking on the Energy Crisis

Our energy resources are under pressure. We are taking too much coal, oil, and gas from our Earth, and someday soon we are going to run out. Scientists are racing to create renewable energy resources, but it is a race against time. Can science win this fight?

SIDING WITH THE SUN

Scientists have already developed solar panels that can power buildings and machines. Solar panels use the sun's energy to make electricity. However, solar panels are only effective in hot and sunny places. Can scientists find ways of making solar energy an effective energy source worldwide?

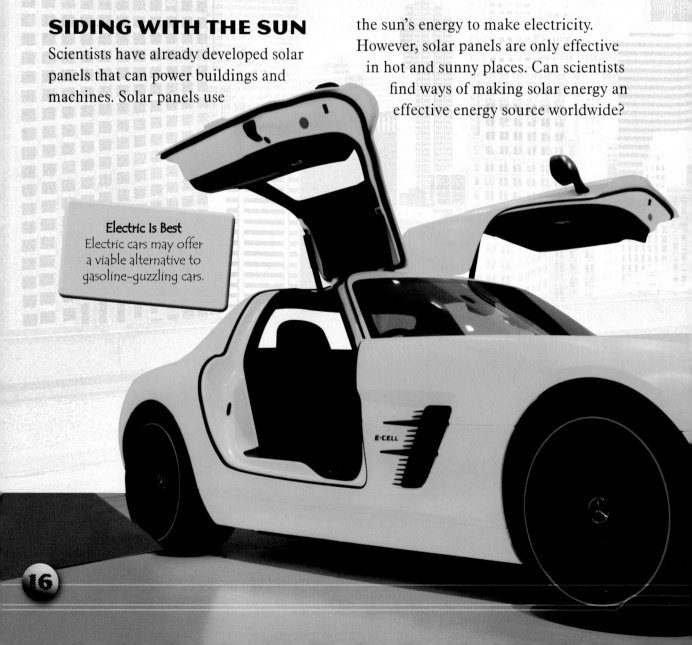

Electric Is Best
Electric cars may offer a viable alternative to gasoline-guzzling cars.

E-CELL

COMING CLEAN

Science has a dirty fight on its hands. The gasoline we use to power our cars is emitting fumes that contribute to global warming. We will also eventually run out of this natural resource. Scientists have developed biofuels—fuel made from plants—to try to solve the problem. This fuel is clean and does not pollute the planet. However, large areas of farmland are required to grow enough plant crops to make biofuel, which means that less farmland is available for much-needed crops. Can science find a solution?

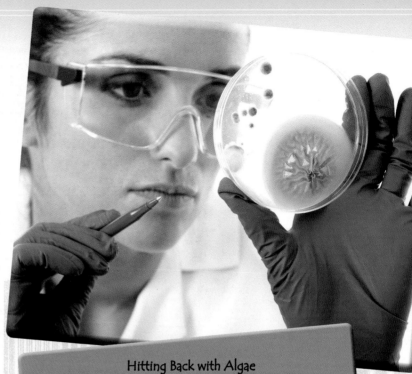

Hitting Back with Algae

Scientists are experimenting with algae fuel. Algae are tiny plantlike living things that live in water. As they grow, they take in carbon dioxide and produce oxygen. Biofuel made from algae may be a clean energy source. This is because the balance of carbon dioxide remains the same—algae soak up the same amount of carbon dioxide that they then release when they are burned. The amount of carbon dioxide in the atmosphere remains the same.

Winning or Losing?

Some scientists believe the electric car is the future. These cars can be powered by electricity rather than gasoline and emit no dangerous fumes. However, electric cars are still expensive to buy. There are also very few electric stations where drivers can refuel. These cars could solve many of our transportation energy problems, but only if we can make them more affordable.

Reducing Energy Use

Science can help us to fight back against climate change by reducing the amount of energy we use. Energy consumption harms the environment, and it costs money too. What can science do to help us save energy, and will it be enough?

Amazing Insulator
Aerogels are some of the world's best insulators. They are used by NASA to insulate spacesuits against the extreme cold of space. Currently they are very expensive to produce, but they could play a big role in making our buildings more energy efficient.

SUPER INSULATION

The United States Energy Department estimates that heating and lighting for buildings makes up nearly 40 percent of our energy use. One of the best ways to save energy is to keep heat from leaking out of our buildings. Insulating materials allow very little heat to pass through them. When they are installed in attics and walls, they keep more heat inside our homes. Home insulation can be made from glass fiber, wool, and even recycled newspapers.

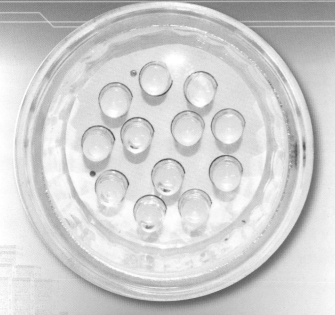

LIGHT FANTASTIC

Governments in many countries have banned the production of filament lightbulbs. Filament lightbulbs are very inefficient. Of the energy they receive, they convert only 10 percent to light and the remaining 90 percent to heat. Low-energy fluorescent bulbs are up to six times more efficient than filament lightbulbs. Their use is becoming widespread. In 2012, scientists unveiled a lightbulb that used special light-emitting diodes (LEDs) to provide light. This bulb used less energy than filament lightbulbs, but there was a problem—each bulb cost around $60!

Reducing the Cost
The cost of LEDs will become cheaper as more and more people buy these energy-efficient lightbulbs.

Winning or Losing?

Electronic equipment such as phones, televisions, and computers currently make up 15 percent of all energy use. This may triple by 2030. Thanks to science, many of today's electrical appliances use much less energy than in the past. And new gadgets are invented all the time.

The Search for Fossil Fuels

While scientists research new energy sources, coal, oil, and gas are still likely to be our main energy sources for many years to come. Advances in science are helping big energy companies to find fossil fuels in places that were once far too difficult to reach.

To the Limit
Drilling for oil in the frozen Arctic tests equipment and workers to the limit.

DEEP-SEA OIL

Many oil deposits are found beneath the ocean floor. For a number of years, oil wells could only be drilled in shallow water. Since the 1990s, oil exploration has started in the deep ocean, in water up to 9,840 feet (3,000 m) deep. The oil rigs' engines are linked to global positioning systems (GPS). This allows the rig to automatically be kept in the right place. Robot submarines take care of drilling equipment and pipes in the extreme cold and intense pressure on the ocean floor.

FRACKING

Gas companies have developed a process called fracking. In this process, water and chemicals are pumped into layers of underground rock to extract gas. The water must be pumped at a very high pressure to break up the rock. Anti-fracking campaigners claim that fracking pollutes water supplies and can cause earth tremors.

OIL SANDS

The sands of central Canada are mixed with a thick tar that is also a form of oil. This mixture can be separated and made into liquid oil. This involves heating and treating the oil sands, using lots of energy. This process makes oil sands a very expensive source of oil.

Winning or Losing?

Extracting oil from oil sands uses up much more energy than normal oil extraction. It also creates even greater carbon dioxide emissions. Another problem is that water is needed to extract the oil from oil sands. Once it has been used, the water must be stored in huge ponds because it is extremely dangerous to the environment. Oil sands have also been found in Utah in the United States but the oil has not yet been extracted because of these problems.

On the Surface
Oil sands in Canada are providing a source of oil that does not require heavy underground drilling.

21

Cleaning Up the Mess

Science plays a key part in clearing up the mess created by use of energy sources such as fossil fuels.

CARBON CAPTURE

Most of the world's power plants still run on coal, pumping out carbon dioxide and other pollutants into the atmosphere. One possible solution to this is Carbon Capture and Storage (CCS). This process prevents these gases from entering the atmosphere. It captures and stores them underground. This is an attractive option for many people because it would allow us to continue using fossil fuels. However, capturing all the carbon released by power plants would be expensive.

Breaking Through

Microorganisms eat oil and clear up oil spills on land. Bacteria eat the oil, and, once their food source is gone, they die off. Scientists are growing microorganisms to see if they can help solve oil spills and other messy pollution problems.

Dirty Travel
The pollution released by aircraft and other vehicles contributes to the harmful carbon dioxide in Earth's atmosphere.

OIL SPILL DANGER

Science leads the fight to deal with oil spills and the damage they do to animal and plant life. Powerful chemicals can be used to clean up oil on the surface of the ocean. The chemicals cause the oil to separate into small droplets. The droplets spread out more quickly in the water and become diluted. However, many scientists are concerned that these chemicals are actually more harmful to wildlife than the oil itself.

PLASTIC PROBLEM

Crude oil is not only made into fuels for all kinds of vehicles. It is also the basic raw material for plastics and other man-made materials. Plastics do not break down naturally. Scientists have discovered that the number of plastic fragments in a large area of the Pacific Ocean called the Great Pacific Garbage Patch is now 40 times larger than it was just 40 years ago. This is having a very harmful effect on wildlife that live and swim there.

Clearing Up
The clear-up operation after the 2010 oil spill disaster in the Gulf of Mexico may continue for years to come.

Clean Cars

Fossil fuels are used in transportation, from family cars to large ships and passenger aircraft. They are a major source of pollution. Scientists are working hard to find an alternative to the internal combustion engine used in vehicles, which runs on fossil fuels.

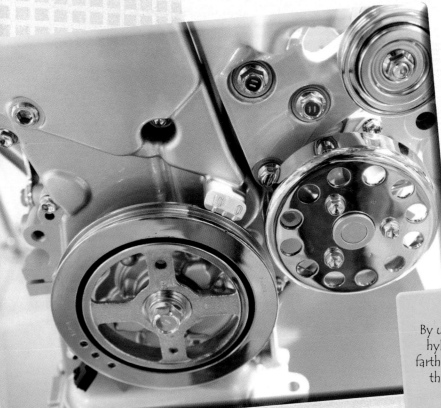

Hybrid cars have both a regular internal combustion engine and also an electric motor. The engine charges the motor, which is used when the car needs extra power to go uphill or when stopping and starting on city streets.

Farther on Less
By using an electric motor, hybrid cars can go much farther on each gallon of gas than conventional cars.

HOPES FOR HYDROGEN

The fuel of the future could be hydrogen. Inside a hydrogen fuel cell, hydrogen reacts with oxygen and releases energy and water. This makes hydrogen a very clean fuel. Hydrogen fuel cells have been used to run vehicles such as buses. There are some drawbacks to consider. Developing the technology for using hydrogen in cars, such as building refueling stations, is very expensive. Most hydrogen on Earth is stored within other substances, such as water. Energy is needed to separate it from these substances before it can be used in vehicles.

FUTURE TECHNOLOGY

Nanotechnology may be able to help make transportation cleaner. In nanotechnology, individual atoms and molecules are made into structures. These structures are far too small to see with the naked eye. Carbon nanotubes are tiny tubes made up of carbon molecules. They are incredibly light, but much stronger than steel. This form of carbon could be used to make aircraft that use much less energy to fly than current airplanes do.

Winning or Losing?

There is currently around one car for every two people in the United States. However, there is only one car for every 300 people in China. This is changing, though—by 2050 there will be three times as many cars in the world as there are now.

Here Comes the Hybrid
Hybrid cars such as this one are becoming more common on city streets.

Capturing Alternative Energy Sources

The use of hydrogen as fuel for vehicles is just one example of an alternative energy source. Some consider nuclear power to be a good alternative energy source. However, fear of accidents has led many countries to stop investing much money in nuclear power.

Many sources of energy are renewable, such as wind, waves, and tidal energy. Although these could provide a plentiful source of energy, science must first find a way of capturing this power.

WIND POWER

Wind turbines spin when the wind blows. The turbines generate electricity, which is sent to homes and businesses. They are becoming more common in countries where the winds are strong and fairly constant, such as Denmark and other Scandinavian countries.

Big Energy Supply
Denmark gets 20 percent of its electricity supply from using wind power.

WATER TO THE RESCUE

Moving water is another source of energy. River water can be trapped behind a hydroelectric dam. When the water is released, it flows through turbines. The turbines generate electricity. Scientists are trying to find new ways of generating electricity by capturing the energy of ocean waves and tidal flows.

CATCHING THE TIDES

The tides of the world's oceans and seas move back and forth every day. A tidal barrage is one way of converting the energy of tides into electricity. There are only a few working tidal barrages, however. Scientists believe that a barrage across the Severn Estuary in the United Kingdom could provide 15 percent of the country's energy needs. Environmental campaigners are concerned about its impact on wildlife.

Reducing the Cost
Dams can generate a lot of electricity. However, the water behind the dam makes a lake, which can disrupt plant and animal habitats.

Winning or Losing?
Use of renewable energy is growing all the time, but it still only makes up around 8 percent of all energy used in the United States.

EARTH ITSELF

In volcanic parts of the world, such as Iceland and New Zealand, geothermal power is very important. Beneath Earth's crust, the rock is very hot. Water flows near the rock and becomes heated. If a well is drilled, steam from the hot water rises up through it. The steam can then be channeled through turbines to generate electricity.

Using Solar Energy

Most of the energy we use on Earth has ultimately come from the sun. Heat from the sun creates our weather systems. Wind creates the waves in the oceans. Even fossil fuels are stores of solar energy absorbed by plants and animals millions of years ago. Scientific advances can also help us to use the sun's energy directly.

Simple solar panels use the sun's energy to heat water. In photovoltaic (PV) panels, the sun's energy is converted into electricity, as happens in a solar-powered pocket calculator. These panels can be fitted to individual buildings. They work best in sunny climates. One big benefit is that this solar power does not have to be transported large distances.

Breaking Through

In 2010, a solar-powered plane landed safely after more than 26 hours in the air. It had huge wings that were covered in solar panels. The plane carried a single pilot. Perhaps solar panels could one day help to power bigger aircraft.

CONCENTRATING THE SUN'S ENERGY

Concentrated solar power (CSP) uses mirrors to focus the sun's energy onto a central point that contains a liquid. The focused solar rays heat the liquid to generate electricity. CSP plants need lots of space. Some experts believe that covering part of the Sahara in Africa with CSP plants could provide a great deal of the world's energy needs.

SOLAR POWER PLANTS

In California, workers are building a huge solar ranch. When it is completed, it will provide enough clean electricity to power 64,000 homes. Scientists believe it will stop around 425,000 tons (385,000 tonnes) of carbon dioxide from entering the atmosphere each year. However, the sunniest places are deserts where few people live. The challenge is how to store the electricity from desert solar plants and transfer it to where it is needed.

Power on the Water
Some solar plants are placed on water to maximize the amount of solar energy they capture.

Power for Everything
Solar power can be used for tasks that need little energy, such as charging cellphones.

Chapter Three: Debates and Issues

Most people agree that the energy crisis is one of the biggest issues facing life on Earth. However, not everyone agrees on how serious this crisis is or the best ways of solving it. Science's fight against the crisis raises lots of questions.

WHAT CAN WE DO?

It is easy to see that the world needs to make changes in how it uses energy. It is very difficult to see how each of us can make a difference. After all, there are more than 7 billion people in the world and each of them uses energy. To reduce our use of energy, we can ensure that our homes have proper insulation. We can bicycle or walk when possible, rather than traveling by car. We can turn off lights, televisions, and computers when they are not being used.

Bigger, Not Better
Bigger and more powerful cars use more fuel. Should governments be discouraging people from buying these cars?

NOT JUST US

Ordinary people can make changes, but it is the world's governments and energy suppliers who need to invest money in renewable energy supplies or research new clean cars to replace our old ones.

In the Ring

Greenpeace and Friends of the Earth are environmental pressure groups. They work hard to highlight the problems facing our planet. They put pressure on governments to tackle climate change and invest money in clean, renewable energy. Despite the work of scientists, there is still much disagreement on the best ways to solve the energy crisis.

Changing Attitudes

Abu Dhabi has been described as the world's richest city. This is because of the oil reserves that lie beneath its desert sands. However, Abu Dhabi is not relying on fossil fuels to supply all its future energy. The country has spent hundreds of millions of dollars on the world's largest solar energy plant. This will take advantage of the city's other great natural benefit—almost constant sunshine.

The Fossil Fuel Debate

Oil and gas companies are some of the world's most powerful businesses. They make billions of dollars by finding and supplying fossil fuels. As the world's thirst for oil uses up more and more resources, these companies have started to search for it in more difficult places. They have drilled in the freezing waters of the Arctic Ocean and found ways to refine oil sands to make oil.

A BETTER WAY?

Environmental groups and scientists argue that these new technologies are not the answer to the energy crisis. If our use of fossil fuels continues to grow, these fuels will become harder and harder to find and more and more expensive to extract. We will face more problems from pollution and we will risk very serious climate change. They argue that the billions of dollars spent on finding new fossil fuels would be better spent on renewable energy.

However, we will use fossil fuels for the foreseeable future so we must develop technology to make them cleaner. This is particularly important because many developing countries in Africa, Asia, and South America are demanding more energy for their growing industries.

Dirty Air, Poor Health
Fumes from traffic cause air pollution in cities, which can damage people's health.

EXIT 24B
Civic Center
Hill Street
ONLY

110
Downtown

EXIT 24C
Dodger
Stadium
EXIT 1/4 MI

A Price Worth Paying?
Public transportation systems use less energy, but they are often less convenient than a car.

TEMPORARY ALTERNATIVE?

Burning natural gas produces less greenhouse gas than burning oil or coal. It could become the main fuel for electricity generation. The main problem is transporting the gas, especially in areas with no gas pipelines. To transport natural gas by ship, it must be cooled until it becomes liquid. This happens at temperatures of −261°F (−163°C). Once it reaches its destination, it is heated or regassified. This whole process is very expensive and uses lots of energy.

Winning or Losing?

Nuclear power may no longer be a viable alternative energy source—many people are worried about its safety. In the year after the Fukushima disaster, only two new nuclear reactor projects started. Some countries, such as Germany, committed to reducing and eventually shutting down all of their nuclear power plants.

Developed Versus Developing Countries

The energy crisis is a global one. Countries around the world all need the same energy resources. Pollution and climate change are global problems. One hundred years ago, the nations that consumed the most energy for homes and industries were the industrial nations of Europe and North America. That is changing because countries such as China and India have become industrial giants. Even the poorest countries of the world are growing their economies, for which they need energy.

A Fair Argument?
People in developing countries argue that they need energy to improve their economy and their living standards.

SAVED BY SOLAR POWER

While developed nations struggle to use less energy, 1.3 billion people in the developing world do not have access to electricity. These countries are often very hot and sunny. This means that they could use solar panels to help power electric lightbulbs instead of using kerosene lamps and to charge the cell phones that are becoming common in places such as Africa.

Solar Solution
By using solar power, developing countries could provide many people with hot water and electricity.

IS IT FAIR?

Developing countries are only just seeing the benefits of science and technology as they grow their economies. The people who live in these developing countries use much less energy per person than the average citizen of North America or Europe. Should they have to pay for the mess created by developed countries? Shouldn't they be given the chance to use fossil fuels to become industrialized in exactly the same way that developed countries have?

Winning or Losing?

Developed countries have a responsibility to change their energy use. These countries are also best able to invest in renewable sources of energy. However, it is not an easy task to persuade people to change their lifestyles or their cars to reduce our dependence on coal and oil.

Chapter Four: The Future

Reducing the amount of energy we use will not become easier in the future. The world's population is expected to grow from 7 billion in 2013 to more than 9 billion people by the year 2050. We can't be sure what science will discover by then, but there are many methods that could help to solve the energy crisis.

FUTURE ENERGY USE

Scientists and engineers can design products for the future that will use less energy. This could include lighter aircraft or home appliances that use less energy. Computers and other gadgets use energy, but they also help us to save energy. People will continue to reduce car journeys by ordering groceries online and working from home.

In with the Old
Bicycles are an old technology, but designing cities for cyclists could make them a big part of the solution to the energy crisis.

THE TRAVEL ISSUE

Many cities have been designed for people traveling by car, with homes, stores, and businesses spread out so they can only be reached by car. If gasoline prices continue to rise, many people will look for cheaper ways to travel and shop closer to home.

THE TRAVEL SOLUTION?

Trains traveling faster than 125 miles per hour (200 km/h) link many cities around the world. Trains travel beneath the English Channel between London, England, and Paris, France, and there is a high-speed service between Beijing and Shanghai in China. These trains are an alternative to air travel between major cities and use much less energy for each traveler than an aircraft. High-speed rail services are likely to spread in the coming years.

Winning or Losing?

New building methods and materials can save energy as homes and offices are built to last for many decades into the future. Buildings can preserve heat using insulation. They can generate their own energy using flexible solar panels included in the design of the building. Any new buildings are likely to feature many energy-saving features in their design.

First Class Travel
High-speed train passengers can travel in comfort between cities.

Future Energy Solutions

Saving energy is important, but the world needs to develop alternative sources of energy if it is to solve the crisis created by our use of fossil fuels.

Desert Energy
Cities in the desert may be able to generate plentiful solar energy in the future.

NEW BIOFUELS

Currently, biofuels can be mixed with gasoline for use in cars. Biofuel is less harmful to the environment than energy sources such as gas. However, as already discovered, the problem is that biofuel crops take up farmland that was previously used to grow food.

Have we replaced one problem with another by growing crops for biofuel? To deal with this issue, future biofuels will be made from alternative materials. There are many options that scientists are exploring, from growing fungi that can help to make biofuel to converting materials such as sawdust into biofuel.

Ultimate Machines
Formula 1 cars use one gallon of gasoline for every 5 miles (8 km). The sport wants to reduce its energy use and to prove that using less energy will not mean slower cars.

Breaking Through

Smart electricity meters can tell customers and energy companies how much energy is being used, when, and what for. This helps companies to plan their electricity supplies so they are not generating more than is needed. In the future, meters may be able to control appliances such as dishwashers and washing machines so they run at times of the day when electricity demand is much lower.

ENERGY STORAGE

While solar or tidal energy can be captured using new technology, it is not always easy to store the energy until it is ready to be used. The deserts or coasts where this energy is generated may also be far away from the big cities where the energy is needed. Hydrogen fuel cells may provide a way of storing energy: in batteries for small gadgets or large plants for power supply.

STREET LIGHTING

Streetlights use energy even if the street they are lighting has no cars on it. Scientists have developed "smart" streetlights that adjust to the brightness of the sky, weather conditions, and also save energy when traffic flows are low. In some cities, such as Chattanooga, Tennessee, all of the streetlights have been replaced with "smart" induction and LED lights. The city is expected to save $2.7 million per year. Solar-powered street lighting is also in place. The lights are able to store solar energy until it is needed.

Endless Energy: Nuclear Fusion

Many people thought that nuclear energy released by splitting atoms would be the answer to the world's energy crisis. This type of nuclear energy is called nuclear fission. Safety concerns mean that many countries are no longer planning to build new nuclear reactors. However, scientists are now working on another form of nuclear energy that could one day solve all of the world's energy problems—nuclear fusion.

Big Ball of Energy
Nuclear fusion is the process that creates the sun's energy.

STAR POWER

Nuclear fusion is different than nuclear fission. Fusion is the process by which the sun generates heat and light. It works by fusing together the nuclei (centers) of hydrogen atoms. To do this, extreme heat and pressure is needed. This fusion releases gigantic amounts of energy, but without the harmful radioactive waste left over by a conventional nuclear reactor.

PROBLEM FREE?

The thought of limitless clean energy makes nuclear fusion very attractive, but there are problems. A fusion reaction requires enormously high temperatures to start it off. As no material can stand this temperature, the hydrogen atoms need to be bonded together by a super-strong magnetic field. These difficulties mean nuclear fusion could be science's greatest test in the fight against the energy crisis.

Harnessing the Sun
The Next Generation Power Plant in Italy is experimenting with enormous structures such as the one above to capture and store solar power.

In the Ring
Albert Einstein (1879–1955) was one of history's most important scientists. He worked out that matter is another form of energy. When two atoms fuse together, they lose a tiny amount of their mass. Mass is a measure of how much matter is in a substance. The mass that has been lost becomes a huge release of energy.

WILL IT HAPPEN?

Nuclear fusion as a major source of energy is still a long way off. Scientists from many countries are working together to build a fusion reactor in southern France. This test reactor will not be finished for many years and, as yet, no one knows if it will work.

The Fight Continues: Is Science Winning?

The search for new sources of oil and coal continues. More power stations are being built to supply developing industries with electricity, and more cars hit the highway every year. Based on these facts, a solution to the world's energy crisis seems a long way off. But there are many reasons for optimism and, if people are committed to solving the problem, change can happen quickly.

Breaking Through

Many areas of science are working to solve the energy crisis. In 2012, researchers developed a device that used a layer of viruses to generate electricity. When a button was pressed, the viruses turned this mechanical energy into electricity. This same principle could possibly be used to generate electricity from regular vibrations, such as the movement of a vehicle or household appliances such as washing machines.

Energy Efficient
There are many ways to improve the energy efficiency of your house.

solar panels

energy efficient lighting

wall-cavity insulation

MAKING PROGRESS

Science is making great progress in developing new technologies that can solve the crisis. New technologies are helping to make renewable energy sources, such as solar and wind energy, a more practical alternative to fossil fuels. Innovations such as carbon capture may help to reduce the environmental impact of fossil fuel power stations. Hybrid and electric cars are starting to appear on highways around the world. New developments such as lighter and more energy-efficient building materials are also playing their part.

Natural News
In many parts of the world, motorcycles are being converted to run on natural gas.

glazed windows

underfloor heating

GLOBAL CHANGE

However, the challenges remain immense. While scientists struggle to find alternative sources of energy, it sometimes seems as though the world's governments cannot agree on any measures to solve the crisis. Global leaders need to agree on the way forward to ensure that science's fight against the energy crisis is not in vain.

The Energy Story

1769
James Watt patents the first modern steam engine powered by coal, beginning the dominance of fossil fuels.

1859
Edwin Drake drills the first commercial oil well in Titusville, Pennsylvania.

1882
Thomas Edison opens the first electric power station in New York City. It is used to power the electric lightbulbs he invented.

1885–86
Karl Friedrich Benz builds the first gasoline-powered car.

1888
Charles Brush uses a windmill to charge batteries in Cleveland, Ohio.

1954
The world's first nuclear reactor opens in the USSR (now Russia).

1988
The IPCC is formed by the United Nations to assess the progress and impact of Earth's global warming.

1997
The Kyoto Protocol is agreed in Japan. Many countries agree to cuts in greenhouse gas emissions. Toyota then introduces its Prius hybrid car in Japan.

2006
China completes the Three Gorges Dam on the Yangtze River, the world's largest dam at the time of its completion. It is capable of supplying as much power as 15 coal-fired power plants.

2010
Deepwater Horizon oil spill in the Gulf of Mexico is the world's worst accidental oil spill.

World energy use jumps by 5.9 percent, the biggest jump in many years, with usage of fossil fuels and other energy sources increasing.

1904
The first geothermal power plant is built in Tuscany, Italy.

1908
Henry Ford produces the Model T, the first mass-produced car for ordinary families.

1947
The transistor is invented, an essential component of most modern electrical devices.

1950
The United States owns 50 million cars and oil overtakes coal to become the country's most important source of fuel.

1950s
Researchers at famous Bell Laboratories develop the photovoltaic cell that could use the sun's energy to drive everyday equipment.

2011
A tsunami hits Japan and causes the Fukushima nuclear power plant disaster.

2012
The world's largest solar power plant opens in Spain. It is the size of more than 200 football fields.

2050
The IPCC estimates that by this year, 80 percent of the energy needs of the 9 billion people on Earth could be met by renewable energy.

Glossary

acid rain rain that has reacted with air pollution to become an acid, which can damage trees, buildings, and animals

algae tiny plantlike living things

atmosphere the layer of gases surrounding Earth

atoms the smallest units or particles of matter

biofuel a fuel made from plant material

carbon dioxide a greenhouse gas that is released when fossil fuels and organic matter are burned

climate the average weather conditions in an area over a long period of time

climate change the theory that Earth's climate is getting warmer and that this is caused by human actions such as the burning of fossil fuels

crude oil the form in which oil is taken from the ground before it is refined to make other substances

evacuate to arrange for people to leave a building or area because they are in danger

filament a thin piece of metal that heats up and glows brightly in an old-fashioned lightbulb

fossil fuels energy sources formed from the decayed remains of living things, including coal, oil, and natural gas

fusion when two things come together to form something new. In nuclear fusion, hydrogen atoms come together to create helium

generates converts one form of energy into another, for example to produce electricity

greenhouse effect the process by which greenhouse gases trap the sun's heat to warm Earth

greenhouse gas gases that absorb heat in the atmosphere

Industrial Revolution the major development of industry in a country, including the making of goods in factories. The Industrial Revolution began in the eighteenth century in Europe and in the nineteenth century in the United States.

insulation a material designed to prevent movement of heat, for example to keep buildings or people warm

internal combustion engine a type of engine in which motion is powered by the burning of fossil fuels with air, as in a car

microorganisms tiny living things, such as bacteria or viruses, that are only visible through a microscope

molecules two or more atoms joined together

radiation harmful particles emitted by materials used in nuclear power generation

radioactive describing a substance that decays over time, releasing particles or radiation

renewable an energy source that can be used again and again, such as wind or solar energy

tidal barrage a structure built across a river or estuary to capture tidal energy

turbines motors, driven by steam, water, or wind power, that generate electricity

For More Information

BOOKS

Challoner, Jack. *Energy*. New York, NY: Dorling Kindersley, 2012.

Hunter, Nick. *Offshore Oil Drilling*. Chicago, IL: Heinemann-Raintree, 2012.

Spilsbury, Richard. *Solar Power*. New York, NY: Powerkids Press, 2012.

Whiting, Jim. *The Science of Lighting a City: Electricity in Action*. Mankato, MN: Capstone, 2010.

WEBSITES

Find out about all of the arguments against the use of fossil fuels and nuclear energy on the Greenpeace website:
www.greenpeace.org

Discover more about ocean pollution at:
www.education.noaa.gov/Ocean_and_Coasts/Ocean_Pollution.html

Follow the lessons on the Department for Energy's website about fossil fuels at:
www.fossil.energy.gov/education/energylessons/index.html

Click the links to the right of the page to uncover fascinating facts about energy at:
www.eia.gov/kids/index.cfm

Publisher's note to educators and parents: Our editors have carefully reviewed these websites to ensure that they are suitable for students. Many websites change frequently, however, and we cannot guarantee that a site's future contents will continue to meet our high standards of quality and educational value. Be advised that students should be closely supervised whenever they access the Internet.

Index